God Save Your Mad Parade

by

austen roye

God Save Your Mad Parade

Poems ©2016 by Austen Roye
facebook.com/austen.roye
all rights reserved by the author

Cover photo by Chandra Alderman
facebook.com/peggy.honeydew

Crisis Chronicles #84
ISBN: 978-1-940996-36-3
1st edition, 2nd printing

First published 6 April 2016
Crisis Chronicles Press
John Burroughs, editor
3431 George Avenue
Parma, Ohio 44134

crisischronicles.com
ccpress.blogspot.com
facebook.com/crisischroniclespress

and he's never on time.

Vincent comes stumbling down the stairs
with his shades on and he's muttering something
about Theo, how Theo never wrote back, how Theo
never cared, not really, no matter how much he said
he did or pretended to and I don't know what to tell
him, this is all so sudden, he's only been living here
a couple of weeks and already he's lost it.   this was
supposed to be good for him and look at him throwing
himself around the room, pitiful, he should be up in the
room I made up for him, working.
Vincent's happy when he's working, it calms
him like nothing I've ever seen, he's not such
an animal when he's got something to tend to.
he's got to keep busy or else he'll wind up
falling down my stairs as he does now.
I fold my arms.
he's been drinking.
I have too, you don't see me bothering
anybody and in my own home this is
happening, who would've thought?
"I'll do it," he says, "don't think for a second
that I won't do it."
I don't say anything.
"I'll go out in the field and do it
all over again! I swear!"
he's crying now, I can see it.
he falls to the floor, lands in his spit
and drops the bottle.
it tips, spills all over the rug and the
rug is white and the wine is red, see,
it'll never come out.
it's empty now, but he picks it up anyway
and sets it upright.
some time passes.   he sobs and sobs.
I don't say a word.
then he looks at me and wipes
his face with his hands.
"sorry," he sputters, "sorry about
the rug."
he gathers himself, stands up,
holds himself upright against

4

the wall.　he's panting.
"I'll be upstairs," he says.
"o.k., Vincent."
on his way up he turns.
"I may have thrown
up in your shoes."
"o.k., Vincent."

ten. twenty. thirty.

they only know exactly
what they don't want,
and when they decide on
something they don't mind
so much it's something like
a bicycle cut in half and set
on fire in the gallery while
everyone drinks mineral
water and watches from
behind the velvet lines.

the abstracts don't sell
since thinking is such hard
work, the performance artists
choke on glitter, it's horrible,
and the lights are on somewhere
around here, only we never see it
and if we ever do, it isn't us who
see it, it's our grandchildren or
their grandchildren, ten twenty
thirty years after they've stuck
the shovel into the heap.

and maybe that's that and
maybe that's just the way
the world works, and with
some luck, in ten twenty
thirty years I'll be behind
the velvet lines holding a
glass and hating everything
in the gallery and knowing
everything about art

which is to know that
all art is
not as good as
not as good as
not as good as
what was and
could've been
could've been
could've been...

as they never do.

she took the crucifix
down from above her
bedroom door and
put it away somewhere,
some place where he
couldn't stare down
at her anymore,
it was unnerving,
nobody needs that
kind of pressure.
she took it down
off its hook and
the roof didn't cave
in, the mirror didn't
break, the earth
didn't open up,
there wasn't the
slightest hint of
tremors in the
ground, not a
single black cloud
and no fires in
any direction that
hadn't been set
deliberately.
she took it down
and was told it was
the principle of
the matter, the
importance of
confessing
your true
self
publicly.
she took it down
and was told
all manner of
frivolous
platitudes,
all that sordid,
sentimental

crap about
a grandmother
in tears all alone
in the sanctuary
with her beads
and mourning
black dress and
how could you
do this to her,
she's too old,
you know how
she is, she won't
let it go, she's
calling her
friends, she's
calling the
priest, she's
up all night
by the candle
chanting at
the ceiling
for your
soul.
but she took it
down and they
all noticed,
everyone
noticed,
they noticed
the cross
for the first
time because
it wasn't
there.

well-to-do.

in my time there's
been all manner of
downfalls pitfalls
upheavals and lies
and natural and
unnatural disasters,
employees in their
morning nothings
eating their own
fingertips in hotel
bathroom stalls,

heads in paper bags
coughing gasoline and
a million rings through
a million noses, skulls
spray-painted on courthouse
walls, inverted crosses
spray-painted on church
walls,

neighborhood watches
holding meetings to lay
out a solid plan of action
over coffee, somebody's
bright idea, and in my time,
which is no time, really, there's
been well-to-do citizens bright
in their Monday suits and ties
stamping seals onto envelopes
to send to the capital,

some guy who ran for
mayor in some nearby
shanty shaking my hand
in a bank lobby, "it's so
nice to meet you, son, you
have yourself a damn good
day, you hear?"

in my time, all pretending

to be so interested in the
weather, in what everybody
has to say, which isn't
much, but enough to pass
the time, all manner of
jobs held and tossed aside
like bad jokes, nothing to it,
balding managers, "and
when you're done with
the garbage come find
me, I've got a project
for you…"
uniforms caked
with the gleam
of fresh grease.

well, hell.

another pair of hands
with five fingers to fill
the gloves won't do it,
two feet to fill the jackboots
won't do it, one head for
the helmet won't do it
and the long-term
ideologies won't
do it, either.

and to have enough
means the end of
everything and to
know complacency
means to give in,
so here's to never
having it, to general
dissatisfaction, to
the next best thing
and the next, if it's
out there.

and you have
yourself a damn
good day.

advisory (!)

and you are never defined
by all the things you don't do
and your being has been
subjected to meaning based
on work ethic, religious
preference, sexual preference,
general occupation, company
kept and dress

and you are never as alone as
you think you are, there at your
desk in your bed in your office
at your window in your closet

and whatever's left of
you is what they're after
and whatever you don't
fight them for you hand
over willingly and it
happens that fast for some,

they'll take anything
they can and run with it
they'll drag it through the streets
they'll stoke it to ashes and scatter
it to the wind
like so much dust
thick enough to make you cough
harsh enough to make you remember
and after that they'll have everything
even your lungs,

and it doesn't stop there
it never does
it goes on and on
as long as you
allow it to.

they'll grind you up
and sell you on the
dollar menu

with a plastic
wind-up toy.

you could so easily
be their
bargain.

a bad one.

who closed the cage door?
what's with all this rust?
how decadent your decay will be.
how many more American processions?
we're running out of flowers.
what's all that noise?
could it be it's finally happening?
is there even enough time to explain
and would anyone understand?
it's all dead space white noise
a general hollow ring
like an oil drum.

all the artists have beards
and order imported beers at the bar
and wander the halls of the hotel
drunk and clutching the walls.
they sit at the window
and think think think
and look off in the distance
'til someone asks them what
they're doing and they
roll a rehearsed line
and everybody around
actually believes this person
is *CONTEMPLATING THE
VOID.*

we're hanging on a
hook in the window.
we're belly-down in
the Sunday dirt.
the next door neighbor
coughs all night.
the switch on the wall
won't turn on the light.

it's actually happening
and it's happening to you
it's happening to us
and it's no question
who's responsible.

jetlagged.

the situation for all its
drab talk wisecracks billboard
spotlight sex book religious
godless shameless self-promotion,
has potential in one way or another,
but from what I've heard you've got
to be standing on a mountaintop
overlooking a foreign landscape
at sunset to realize this.

just read Ernest or Jack or
Mark, they'll tell you.   read
Allen or Walt or Dylan.

imagine them all sitting bonfire
semicircle peyote high, agreeing
with each other.   imagine them sitting
around discussing the cosmos and the
depths of the unconscious soul.

imagine all that crap spilling out
in conversation like that and all of
them nodding and reveling in the
idea that maybe they know something
the world doesn't.   it's gotten more
and more difficult to believe them.
I go back and read these articles,
these interviews, these poems, these
short stories, these biographies where
these drunken bearded intellectuals
discuss their extensive travels to Europe
in the fifties; London Greece Africa
Italy, anywhere.

they talk about these things and they
always want to tell you about the night
scenes and the sunsets and the faces
passing by the bar windows the café
windows, the view from the balcony,
ships in the harbors...

I read these things, I hear these stories
and wonder *how the hell they did it*.
freelance deadbeat poets splitting
the ocean, transatlantic boxcar plane
ride train ride, always going somewhere
that isn't America, falling in love with
brown-eyed Brazilian girls, the same ones
who want to tell you all about how little
they had, how they suffered, the loss the
loss the loss, always.

how the penniless drunk with no support
ends up on the Eiffel Tower with a blonde
in a champagne glass dress, I'll never know.

it's becoming more and more difficult,
though I want to believe them.   I want them
all to myself, the versions of them I've created.
but they're different people on different days,
even in death.   even in death there's no escaping
change.   imagine that: an inconsistent death.

life or death, inside or out, mountains or walls,
there's potential.   the next step is deciding what
to do when the old bones don't speak the way
they used to.

what happens next?

that's it.

the dimwits.

their faces like the cracks in the coffee cups
mouths that leak like faucets
dimwitted thoughtless old geezers in their teens
kids born with the oldest souls around.

they know something's going on here
they've got the strangest feeling
and they write letters to their editors
to tell them about this feeling,
how they can't quite figure it out
and even if they could
they wouldn't know how to react to it.

and the trucks come to pick up their garbage
the dishwasher scalds his hands on their dishes
and goes home to three kids and no door hinges
a wife out on the town with friends or anyone.

he knows something's going on here
he's got the strangest feeling
and he tells himself all about it
in the bathroom mirror,
and he knows it, knows all about it,
and he's fully aware of his options,
unsteady as they are.

if there is a soul,
this one's dragging its knuckles
through the mud on its way to
the post office to send off
the electric bill
three weeks late.

he knows all about it.
he doesn't know a thing.

he only knows
tomorrow is
Tuesday.

lipstick rim.

the man envisions
himself in foreign
countries with exotic
women rowing his boat
toward the marble fountains
and waking up blissful and
hung over but well-rested
in his wide open
bed with white sheets,
tossed about in all the
right places and the hair
of this girl or that spread
over a lace pillow,
her glass red at the bottom,
lipstick rim.
envisions himself
upright now with coffee,
smoking a very thin cigarette
she rolled for him.

the man plans his day
according to the whims of
his carelessness.   he opens
himself to the light and wind
of the alley, the brush of the
skin on his own, her breath
on his neck.

he is in
complete
control.

for all of this,
the man forgets the
simple things;

he so easily forgets
he's a vulture, that he
is waiting for her to
give up, that his intentions
are purely animalistic,

how simple an act it is
to be a decent
human being.

the man forgets these
things, his confidence
is too high, his world is
too wide, his intentions
are wrapped
in velvet.

the man is quick
to lose sight of
himself

the woman has
her mirror
always.

may.

the days have been unreasonable.
servicing the public for a living
so easily makes one forget there
ever was anything else out there.
you lose the last bits of interest
you ever had in people;
people so easily become something
other than people under those
conditions.
they become liabilities
numbers
minutes
seconds
faces with mouths that
are always
always
asking questions.
it does something to you
to sit through it day after
day, and some people
do it for years,
some get lucky,
move on to the
next one.

I've lived in this house
for over a year now,
behind the blind
rooster's coop;
he spends all day
screaming at the sun,
much like we do.

and it's not intolerable
necessarily, at times the
days are harmless,
they just pass like
any number of
numb hours.
there are ways,
one finds ways,

one invents ways,
because if you didn't
take the time to at
least invent your
way out, that rooster
would've had an
unfortunate
accident
a long time
ago.

and anyway,
people are all animals
at best,
the only thing that sets
us apart from the rest
of them are our
interests.

so,
another day done,
an unreasonable one
at best,
and the rooster
already watching
the sun
much like
we do.

that said,
I make for
my
imaginary
exit.

walking lobotomy.

stumbling afternoon idiots
they really think they're onto something
they really think they've got it figured out
they come with their life-concepts packed
away into gift-wrapped boxes
ribbons and bows
their dumb, empty conversations
they turn to one another:
hello, how are you?
well, I'm fine
how are you?
fine, fine
and that's if they say
anything at all.
they come mumbling to themselves
teeth eroded by oceans of coffee
tides coming and going for decades
and they talk about their children
and about how much more intelligent
more ambitious more athletic more interesting
they are compared to other children
and they talk about rain
and sunlight and wind and heat and cold
but never in any context other
than simply acknowledging
the fact that these things exist.
lunch hour traffic passes by the
window and they wish they
wouldn't drive so fast
they wish it would rain
they wish it wouldn't rain
they wish the new restaurant
didn't put cilantro on everything
and the service isn't so great either,
the waitress didn't even smile
not even once.

some people.

you can't rush art.

sorry, Johnny
it's a long fall from here
and I just don't have it in me
to look down.   this is dangerous
work you've got going here and
I'll leave you to it, as much as I'd
like to stick around to see how it
all turns out.

you've got everybody in town
convinced but yourself and I can
see you're still trying to put things
together in your head, no shame in
it, it's a big decision and it's one
you've got to make yourself.

and I don't mean to rush you
but we've been out here for two,
maybe three hours and the stores
close at eleven on weeknights,
I've got work at eight and you do
too and I'm all out of sick days,
they're gonna start docking my pay.

the mail's stacking up on the
kitchen counter, the fridge is out,
I'm keeping my goods in the sink
with ice cubes, when they come to
the door I pretend I'm not in but they
just ring and ring like they know I'm
there, you can't imagine the pressure
I'm under.

they're gonna come with pitchforks
soon enough, they'll drag me out by
my ankles, hang me upside-down in
the square, they'll leave me for the
buzzards.

I can't stay, Johnny, I just can't,
they'll be looking for me soon,

I've got to get going, the sun's
setting, they always come out in
the evening, I don't know why,
it's just what they do.

call me later,
let me know how things
turn out.

I won't answer the first time,
but just wait a minute and
I'll call back.

it's safer that way.

figurine.

the sound comes barreling down the hallway
the bed sheet rolls back like a wave
the floor's been paced beyond capacity
soon you'll be in the downstairs neighbor's
living room wondering what happened.
they all go rushing around screaming at steering wheels.
somewhere a girl's trying on a new dress,
she's deciding she isn't sure,
she's deciding she can't stand it.
somewhere the boy's got his eyes closed
and in all that black there's legs forever and
flesh-hips under lace and porcelain teeth
to compliment the glass eyes that glow
when the light's just right.
all the others fail in comparison to his
mannequin and always will, all the same
the ones who remind him of it will do.
all we know is as we know it is to be
only what would be better under any
other circumstances and to hell with the moment,
hindsight is easier, it takes liberties, it spreads it
all out in front of you like a tabletop.
your bed heavy with dust, skinless hands
and somewhere her hair in rolls spilling on and on.
she's there somewhere and she's all yours
you own her
you built her and it's all right in front of you
when the light's just right
but even the light is something
you've manufactured.
the sound comes rushing down the hallway,
throws your door open, the bed sheet in the air,
gets caught in the ceiling fan, the blades snap off,
come crashing down the light bulbs pop and
scatter sparks the books fly from the shelf closet
door opens clothes torn from hangers drawers
flung open the air rotating pages and
shoestrings and one final brilliant triumphant
unmatched blast of sound and with the last
white pop the lights
go out.

take two.

it unfolds sporadically
and in no particular order
starts to divide and
in a way
organize
the mental and emotional
status of people
and the selection is
consistently based on
temperament
awareness and
overall calm
and the dividing line
is just time or
a lack thereof
and there's nothing
else, we just
wake up
have coffee
go to work
and somewhere
in all of that
fall into
the filter.

wait a second
what in god's name am I talking about?
this is all trailed off into some
desperate Freudian lecture.

this is
crap.

I'll be the first to admit it.

I'm not saying anything that the
world doesn't already know.
we all know about time,
that's nothing new and it
sure as hell isn't interesting.

just time and awareness
and nothing else?

horrible.

this piece shouldn't exist
but I can't think of a reason
to stop it now, so I'll try
again:

no more time metaphors,
that isn't poetry,
that isn't anything.
that's a wet cigarette.

to hell with time,
I should've said *decision!*
that's it!
decision!
it was all rolling along
and it started to trail off into
nonsense and it was just hanging
there; what's the word I'm
looking for?

decision.

the rest of it, the part
about falling into the
filter and all of that,
I'll stand by that.

that line felt alright
and it's still up there
so feel free to climb
back up to it and
try it out again.

but the rest of this,
this piece,
it's all dust
ashes, tin cans,
bottle caps,

general American refuse,
no matter what the critics
or the professors or
anyone says.

don't believe a
word of it.

go
read
Tolstoy.

trains.

wide awake and unsettled, maybe a little angry
maybe too much quiet in the grand scheme
maybe too much familiarity with the sight
and smell, or too much time huddled in
all of it, the quiet and everything, locked
away, just me and my headache...

good evening, how's everything? is that a
fact?   I tell you what, that's just about the
most interesting thing I've heard anyone say
all day and what's that?   the tulips?   yeah,
they're coming in nicely this season, I just
hope the heat doesn't do them in before
the wind does, you know?   what's that?
oh, she's fine, just fine, going about her
business, nothing new and isn't that just
hilarious?   isn't it?   did you see in the
paper that poor man died?   hit by a train,
they said, only forty-two years old, shame.
he used to deliver the paper with his daddy
before school, I remember, isn't that
something?   isn't it?   dead at forty-two,
mercy.   that really is something.

no sirens at night anymore,
not since the sun came out.
that ship has sailed.
it's unnerving, all of this, somebody's
following me around, that's what it
is.   I'll write him into this to see if
he's reading over my shoulder...
maybe he'll react...

...I see you back there,
you spineless sack
of festering
shit....

...nope.

no response.

maybe he's on break.
I'll try again later.
he's not going to
get away with this.

maybe not angry
maybe only disinterested,
disinterested in everything
but creating characters
to curse at in
these little
snapshot
narratives
if that's what they are.

somebody tell me.
I don't have a clue.

it can't wait;
I'm going after him,
the sneaky bastard.
no problem.

I created him.

the night is
entirely
mine.

two. thousand. eleven.

I wake up
go to the sink to brush
and all my teeth are
wiggling
like bowling pins,
the roots have shriveled up.
I'm careful, I only run the
brush lightly over the tops
of them to get that stale,
unconscious taste
out of my mouth.

it doesn't work,
they all pop out,
scattered marbles on the
countertop, all gone.
every last one of them.
I scoop them up,
drop them in the
toilet and flush.

they'll go farther
than I have.

I smile in the mirror
all flesh pink gums,
and I think,
so this is what it's
like to grow old.

you dwindle down
to nothing, it's a long
time getting there but
it happens.   the body
breaks down as it was
designed to do.   you
shrink into yourself
gradually, you barely
even notice until
something like this
happens, until your

hair's in your hands
your skin's stretched
into waves, your facial
features reduce to one
ongoing, unorganized
indention...

that's what
happens.

you look at yourself
and you think
well, hell

today I'm
twenty-four.

on going home.

the boss said I had no common sense.

I clocked out. the light changed, I moved
forward, we all stopped and slid to the
shoulder to let the ambulance pass.
brain-dead day of days, what's with all the noise?
I could so easily be storming through the reds
and yellows, skidding the yields, wasting the stops,
not all this confined resolve to tick the
turn signal to death.

something's happening here.   it's over, the siren goes
dissonant the way they do in motion, we all roll back
out onto our own respective sides of the line.   home is
that way, work is the other way.
I know these ways well.

turn right, you keep going you'll run into an
Italian place, a bar with cathedral ceilings to your
left, family-style seating on your right.
the bartender's name is Rocky.

skip the bar, head straight on the same road,
I used to live out there by the open field, you
may remember.   I barely do.   I sketched every
staircase in the place with my bare fingertips.
wonder how I did.   weird, thinking about it.

last weekend, other side of town, crashed sick
at midnight, a veteran blackout if any, leaning on
years of accidental eventual inevitable intentional
experience.   she lied down beside me before she
had to leave for the night, I didn't remember.

but the boss said I had no common sense,
called me an easy target, I remember that,
and Rocky the bartender, I remember him too.
he's got a round face, dark hair cut short, a little
on the heavy side but not fat, just broad.   the boss
has a face like a sleepless bloodhound, heavy features,
laughs at things that aren't funny, good at it too,

good with people. not so fond of me.   but I get it,
there's not much of a workspace, close quarters,
understood.

I'll get the ax soon enough and when I do
I'll have no choice but to try to find the poetic
aspects of ordinary things.   time allows these things
when you have plenty of it.

I'll write ten thousand pages.

imagine it: hardback, pressed and bound;
bad, bad writing.   time allows those
things too.

I pull up at the house, park, get out.

that's Wednesday.

one before they take me.

I'm up late the night before an early-start workday
and I know better, I should've been sleeping hours
ago, but something isn't quite falling into place tonight
and I spent the day behind my desk feeling generally
sick with the most farfetched, the most absurd imaginary
circumstances...I invent my hell...in the quiet it lights up
and puffs smoke in my face, I watch it all unfold and grab
my guts, it's horrible. it opens up and I take the stairs
down into the bowels of it. everybody's hell is different.
today mine was strictly visual, strictly mental. I was
disgusted at the sight of it. it was like a reel of scratched
film with no sound. the scenes didn't follow much of a
plot, since I was the one putting the thing together,
but it was a montage of all the things that could have
happened while my head was turned for a moment,
in all matter of things. I felt like taking an early lunch
break and coming back cackling-mumbling-stumbling
DRUNK. they'd fire me, sure. or maybe I'd get lucky,
they seem like the sympathetic type, maybe they'd
drive me home, tell me to sleep it off, take the next
day off, why not? get yourself together, we're here
for you, friend, sure, take a week, take two! no
insurance? don't worry, go see a shrink, find a
good one, all on our dime! you're a valuable member
of this company and we like to keep our employees
in tip-top shape, it's good for morale and we as a
business know that you're more than a number
or a pawn or a cog or a set of hands. you're a
person, damnit, a human being with real needs
and feelings and well, we just want you to know
we're thinking about you and we're praying for
a quick and efficient recovery...I've got to be
back behind the desk at eight in the morning,
in the proper attire, reflecting the proper mood,
hello, good morning, how are you today, oh, isn't
that lovely, thank you, have a good day and all
that early morning neighborly crap we spoon feed
one another at certain times of day. I think I'll
go to bed now and think of something else, I'll
play a different film, this time with the sound on,
and I'll rise with the sun, I'll beat the alarm

before it has a chance to scream at me and
shatter it all...I think I'll try inventing something
else this time, something with a little more
soul to it.   sure.   then I can watch that roll
by and when I slip into it, I can carry it
down with me.   sounds nice.

lackluster snapshot.

it's coming up out of
the grave I buried it in
red-eyed and toothless
hands like forest fire branches
up out of the hole to drag
itself to my door to peer into
my window while I sleep
not dreaming of it not
dreaming of anything
but it doesn't make its
move not yet it's coming
up out of that hole in broad
daylight only the drivers and
ditch-diggers don't notice
the police cars just pass by
no lights or sirens it's out
there I know it is and I've
got a plan

well, it isn't much of
a plan, but it's all I've
got.   this is as good as
it gets after nine hours
work.

here
goes:

I raise myself up out of my seat
take the white pill and wait
then it happens, I drift out into it
I'm sinking
I'm going
straight
down
slowly
overboard and
undercurrent
down.

I sit back down

spin the chair around
face the window
and stare
back.

damn.

all I have to do is keep going
and really, how difficult could that be?
well, we'll see.
all I have to do is put one word after another
my fingers do all the work
all I have to do is sit there and let it happen
but when it doesn't happen
and when it's not so simple
I drag it around with me everywhere
and it's heavy.
so I look around and wonder
what now?
how do these things work?
where do I begin?

Jesus Christ.

I could be rolling a cigarette in the shade
on some sprawling tree-lined campus
watching the girls walk by talking
about this weekend or the last,
sitting in the back row watching the clock,
opening a beer back at my place
then another,
brilliant, all-in and generally
not giving a damn
but open to
everything.

keep going.

a single light in the shattered dark
ashtray bottles in a grinning window
some pearl-snap bastard shoves me at the party
dead drunk stumbling walk back to the building
three in the morning
they all go home with their catches
and skin each other alive on the chopping blocks
the mattress springs uncoil and tear through
music in the next room slaughters the walls
red-eye dead-eye

sleep like cinder blocks
when the morning
breaks screaming.

the sound would've stuck with me
I would've been someone else completely
too many variations to count
any time or place.

the alarm goes off.

watercolors.

I'll send it out.
yes.
I'll feed the birds to the
envelopes and let them
swallow them up, gulp,
a gurgle like a tilted beer
bottle high tide against a
one-ton gullet, down she
goes and out, too, out
there into the wild of it all,
so many of them still falling
down the shoots into the
bins, gulp, chew, swallow,
forever and again.

I'll send it to its haunted
attic, its electric mainframe,
its neon casket in holy hell
of all our oblivions, and I'll
wait for it, my little carrier
pigeon, to come flapping
back on one and a half
wings, to spill its guts
onto my desktop and
tell me all about the
state of things.

I'll fold 'em up, toss 'em
out the window and up
into the manmade wind
the ocean didn't whisper
in our way, and of it'll go,
the end and beginning of
so many
what's-that-over-there's
and
who-did-what-to-who's
and
what-now-to-where-and-when's.

To go up and over

north for the oncoming
icicle teeth and mad wind
cascades like so many
still-life paintings crucified
forever on the walls of the
Museum of Moderns,
no flash photography.

citizen.

the laureate
providing a public reading
on behalf of a national
tragedy
will look out at his audience
and see only
the mass grave
the bomb falling
the cross-fielded hill
but they rarely ever
call him or her
up from the ranks
to provide the service
their title requires
since in such a
circumstance
any prose or poem
will fall short in
comparison to
the national
platitudes or
the twang single
spun dizzy on the radio
that everyone must
rise for and only
a traitor wouldn't
appreciate...remove
your cap...on and on...
the laureate holds
a heavy obligation
toward his nation
and must be more
than a writer in any
sense, but a patriot,
too, staying inside
the national lines,
void of all agenda
but THE agenda...
so, there laureate,
for all the pomp and
medals and checks

provided, an
expectation in tow,
may as well be
skipping stones
across a
manmade
lake.

we sure was something.

mercy
take a look at us we were stronger
in our twenties weren't we?
his drab features compliment the tall
socks, thick rimmed glasses, he's talking
to me, bloodhound face dragging the floor,
bless his heart.
we sure was something back when they
used to let us run wild through town and
we never did nobody no harm either.   look
at 'em now, there ain't nothing left for nobody,
the kids are all too high on medicines anyway,
what with the parents rather wantin' 'em high
than to have to step up and be a parent is all
I'm saying.
now his hands are on the desk, what's left of
them and I'm out of coffee, he won't just leave
already.   what a shame to say so, how I wish
he would, I want him out of here, away from me,
he hasn't bathed, he looks ragged but everybody
knows him to be well-to-do, he's got money
somewhere, people seem to know that.   I don't
know a thing, only he's still here gnawing on me.
he wants the president impeached but he won't
say so directly.   he drops hints.
the president, he says, wants us all in the
poorhouse, and he's gonna do whatever he's got
to do to put us there.   he's frustrated, I can tell.

politics always lights a fire under an old man's ass.

he stops to catch his breath, coughs, looks around.
he's winding down.   he says, didn't mean to offend
nobody, and he also says, I mean you may have
voted for him and that's ok, and I say it's alright
and I also say, no problem.   I don't know why that
comes out: no problem.   sounds stupid.   he tells me
to have a good day and turns to leave.   he saunters
out, bowlegged, his pants hiked well up above his
navel.   I hop up out of my seat and break for the kitchen.

I wonder how many cigarettes I have left.

en vivo.

they're rallying themselves against the
morning mass, hordes of them shrouded
and neck-tied and caffeinated, they've all
got voices and they all use them but they
all say the exact same words at the exact
same time and it only sends a message as
far as the ceiling and bounces back to no
end, just a two hour shouting match
with a wall.

that's all dandy, but outside it's something
else, they're expecting rain, they're coming
out of their caves and holes to see a hijacked
sun, they're whipping themselves in their
basements, beating their breasts, old
testament.

soon executions will be all the rage,
just you wait, give it a year or two.
old enough to snatch a purse, old
enough to face the gallows!   on camera!
coming at you live from town central,
it's Friday night and what a night it is
for an execution!   so and so, age so and
so, caught having an affair with his wife's
best friend!   the disgruntled lover is standing
by, warming up to pull that lever, let's go
courtside for the pre-death report!

give it a year or two.
they'll put
anything
on television.

they're probably filing out now, the horde,
heading out to all the same restaurants to
order so many chicken fried steaks.   the
dishwashers will contend with pillars of
plates caving in the ceiling tiles.

tomorrow can't be all that dreadful,
it hasn't happened yet.

until then.

clarity.

we're the bastard sons of an electric generation!
we're a mob of illegitimate sons and arbitrary
daughters!
we're going to outlive the Mayan ruins!
we're full speed and breakneck!
we're out and open!
we're carrying torches to hell!
we're legion!
and god
we're bored.

the clerics are adrift with their candle-wax
choreography
the books cough dust onto the black ash pulpit
the bells are pounding one another into iron sheets
the sparks crack wild in all that ceremonious black.

what a drab dull thing your war was
maneuvers and bayonets.
we've got liquid flames!
we've got HQ's on the moon!
we can shoot light through a man's
skull from a birds' nest in Wyoming!
it's easy!
we don't go to war no more!
we go on vacation!
and everybody comes back well-to-do!

trim those wicks!
we can't die!
it's all over!
turn down the sheets!
make up the guest bedroom!
we're on our way
and we're here
for the weekend!

all rights reserved.

every writer is
more or less obsessed
with the concept of time,
not only because it dictates
such a majority of our lives,
but because it, like so many
things, is well beyond our
control, as much as wind and
rain...the best you can do is
carry an umbrella...

every writer
repeats every writer,
we're professional mimics,
we've simply exhausted all
the topics, our resources are
tapped, there are only new
ways of saying old things...

I better start copyrighting
every word I use...

these are all mine now,
you can't have them...

perhaps if everyone else
was so business savvy...

this can't be.... can it?

the only thing more
disturbing than beating
a dead horse is trying to
revive it...

and the innovators,
they all slipped on banana
peels and fell face-first into
genius, and some of them
ran with it, cashed in, some
disregarded it, some piled

stones in their pockets and
strolled into the river...

but perhaps more
often than not, more
than anything, every
writer can't help writing
about every
writer...

backbone.

don't leave
it's too cold here
everything reminds me
of the fence
the wall
the steel
the train station
and I could
I could
I could
go
I've got a job
a few dollars
there are tickets
that admit people
into cables & cars
people ride wires
to places that
aren't here
I could be
could be
could be
one of them
I'll come up to you
ask if this seat's
taken
and if not
would you mind?
we could stare
at our laps
pretend to scan
magazines
newspapers
scenery
'til the brakes engage
and we screech
to a stop
steady
hats & cases
we could go
you to yours

and me to mine
not a word.

sun bleached.

back home comatose
after all day babbling
past three nights
spit beer cans obscenities dry
dawn, end of the day the month
the year;

they trample one another
in the streets it's all vain
all knowing all infinite and
between window panes my
face sleepless, heavy-featured
cinderblock eyes crack the light
and sound, staring back.

agoraphobic in department
stores, lines out the door;
"you look awful last night was great"
I can't process so just sit and
think the fiction dept. is a close-knit
tangle of professional liars with
hidden agendas while the poets
brood over god awful dandelions
that don't say a damn thing
in public parks and biographers
bury themselves vicariously,
slaves to the old bastard scribes,

but at any rate and for what,
I'm doing it again, not writing
but sitting slumped in a holiday
shop beating the exhausted topics,
rented mules, bleached sand bones,
everybody's spit flying at everybody,
ain't no way I'm goin' downtown
this time 'o day no sir...

I look awful last night was great
the mass goes galloping by...

the weight.

the idea was
write your way out
always has been
write your way out
and they want to know
about your influences
who you've read
who you're reading
and I'm still writing
and still reading too
but one of the most
difficult aspects of
the whole charade
is to continue to do
these things while
remaining unchanged
unshaped unmoved
by the influences
appreciating them
respecting them
for what they are
and were
but moving along
into the next
phase
the next task
leaving them in
their places
respectfully
to remain
as they are
as they were
dragging nothing
behind you
taking nothing
with you
whistling along
the way.

red horse antique shop.

the second floor is the worst
it all creaks underneath you
the footsteps rush up behind you
things fall from shelves and the lights,
they're lanterns the way you think of
a lantern posted down the single aisle,
you turn a corner and there's a mannequin
with a wide-eyed face painted on and she's
wearing a wedding dress from the 1960's,
somehow hard to look at.

I leave her there.

used to be apartments up here,
you can tell.   the halls split into hollow
rooms housing decades of garage junk,
attic crap, basement garbage, dolls with
missing limbs, somebody's prom dress
circa god knows when, the delight and
carelessness of a hundred or more families,
acquaintances, silverware rust, lost pots
pans rival shoe parings unraveled trumpets
weathered drum skins stretched over oval
rims, childhoods piled high, disheveled
adolescences, shreds of dresses,
all lost all home or nowhere.

I stood at the window looking out
and wondering, and warped the wood
beneath me on my way to the
moaning staircase.

the end.

they'd sell your own grandmother's
ashes back to you while the books pile up
unsold unwanted.   but the first editions go
and the leather bound editions go because
they'll add to the décor of the second-floor
study overlooking the lake, right there by
the chair you want people to think you sit
in as you contemplate the scenery,

while they march into cinemas worldwide
to sit there two hours and have shit
shoveled
into their laps,

death rattle of the contemporary composer
sharpening the skill of pressing play and
they buy it, Jesus, how they do,
how they do,
by the millions

the plastic hollowed out legless spineless
sewage spewed and allowed into our homes!
our eyes!   our memories!   willingly!   five gallons
of celebrity spit clearance sale two thousand a
jug, maddening, the mirror images reprint
mulligan redefined slam the microwave door
shut on the horse's skeleton, two minutes on
high, still dead but steaming...

it'll have to do, anything beyond that
spectrum out of that boundary beyond
that capacity is too much too strange
too obvious...

the problem with critics being that
people generally believe them...

no room in that inn the pipes are all
busted anyway and there's no room
service, you have to fill your own
ice bucket like some kind of
goddamn animal...

averages.

the plane looks like an anchor overhead.
the only people who care where it's going are on it.
from down here it's only something to look at
while you're stuck in traffic.
people put their hands out the windows and
pluck it out of the sky between their
thumb and forefinger
'til the assembly line heaves
forward and lurches to a stop,
repeat process,
the couple to the right
crack quiet beers and
creep by.

some people are
prepared
for anything.

cavalcade of smoke
cigarettes upturned in
every window
radios up
hell, why not?

the other end of this
comprised of
two nights
three days
forty beers
three hangovers
two coffee cups
two seats
three people
and
one drunk
among them
keeping
count.

opening night at the prisoner's cinema.

they'll go on strike:
the postal workers the sorters
the carriers and never again
another solid bound commemorative
correspondence between two or
more interesting people,
the pigeon is to go the way
of the cassette, so long.
but forward, ok, so many and
maybe myself a part of it pacing
bitching pissed spewing 1940's
documentary footage for the sake
of conservation, integrity of word
sound voice, preserve the six
gallery readings, bring it
back back back
but what's back there is a few
hundred thousand shovels stuck
in a few hundred thousand
commemorative plots.
it's enough to remember,
that's all, if for no other reason
than it must be, it's our only
option, as I sit pompous bored
with headache behind the eyes
scanning Hemingway's letters
thinking, Jesus, how a man
manages to base a literary
career on swordfish and dead
bulls, and outside the kids run
by afternoon yelling, school's
out, work's done, down the
hall the air clicks on, and I
write you and nobody and
everyone else a halfwit letter
of my own to toss in the pile,
everyone living or not looking
back thinking yes, what a
time it must've been
to be alive.

acknowledgments.

we are grateful to the following publications, in which some of these poems originally appeared:

Ascent Aspirations Magazine
Cartys Poetry Journal
Deep South Magazine
Exercise Bowler
Nazar Look

JOHN B. BURROUGHS
EDITOR / PUBLISHER / POET
JC@CRISISCHRONICLES.COM

3431 GEORGE AVENUE
PARMA, OH 44134 USA
WWW.CRISISCHRONICLES.COM
TWITTER @JESUSCRISIS
(440) 315-0426

CRISIS CHRONICLES PRESS
VITAL INDEPENDENT LITERATURE SINCE 2008
CCPRESS.BLOGSPOT.COM   FACEBOOK.COM/CRISISCHRONICLESPRESS